A Prayer Book for Children

Swami Raghaveshananda

Art: Padmavasan

Sri Ramakrishna Math
Mylapore, Madras 600 004

Introduction

Faith in God and prayer to Him are a must for every one for a happy and peaceful life. God created this world. It is He who creates father, mother, brother and sister. He is not far away in the sky. He is in our heart. He knows what is good for us. By praying to Him we can get whatever we want. Prayer helps us to keep in contact with Him. As Sri Ramakrishna says, 'When we put a post card in a letter box, we surely believe it reaches the destination, so also when we pray to God, it surely reaches His ears.' Prayer also purifies our mind and takes us nearer to God. Prayer not only soothes away sorrows and distresses, but makes the mind receptive and responsive at the same time.

Prayer is an appeal to God to make us better persons. Children cannot survive without the love of their parents, even so they cannot survive without the love of God, because God is the parent of parents. Therefore children should cultivate from their young age the habit of praying to God. The constant repetition of the prayers set forth in this book will help the children to gain more and more faith in God.

1. Vedic Prayers

The Vedas are the oldest scriptures in the world. They are four in number — Rig Veda, Yajur Veda, Sama Veda and Atharva Veda. They are the source books for Hinduism. All the other scriptures are based on the Vedas only. The Vedic Prayers are for the good not only of the individual but also for the whole humanity without any distinction of caste or creed. Of all kinds of prayers in the Hindu Scriptures, none are so attractive and impressive as the prayers in the Vedas. They have a direct appeal to the heart. What is the reason for it? These prayers are not mere compositions or writings of any sages. When the sages were meditating, these prayers appeared before their mind's eyes in glowing golden letters. The sages memorised them and taught them to their disciples. So these prayers are God-given. Proper utterance of these mantras bring whatever result one asks for.

ॐ तत्सवितुर्वरेण्यं भर्गो देवस्य धीमहि ।
धियो यो नः प्रचोदयात् ॥ ॐ

Om Tat savitur varenyam
bhargo devasya dheemahi
dhiyo yo nah prachodayaat. Om.

We meditate upon the adorable effulgence of the glowing Sun. May He illumine our intellect.

ॐ सहनाववतु । सहनौभुनक्तु । सहवीर्यं करवावहै ।
तेजस्विनावधीतमस्तु मा विद्विषावहै ॥
ॐ शान्तिः । शान्तिः । शान्तिः ॥

Om Sahanaavavatu. Sahanau bhunaktu.
Sahaveeryam karavaavahai.
Tejasvinaavadheetamastu
maa vidvishaavahaih.
Om Shaantih Shaantih Shaantih.

Om. May He (the Supreme Lord) protect us both (the teacher and the student). May He nourish us both. May our study be thorough and fruitful. May we not hate each other.

ॐ भद्रं कर्णेभिः शृणुयाम देवाः ।
भद्रं पश्येमाक्षभिर्यजत्राः ।
स्थिरैरङ्गैस्तुष्टुवाँ सस्तनूभिः
व्यशेम देवहितं यदायुः ।

स्वस्ति न इन्द्रो वृद्धश्रवाः
स्वस्ति नः पूषा विश्ववेदाः ।
स्वस्ति नस्ताक्ष्यों अरिष्टनेमिः
स्वस्ति नो बृहस्पतिर्दधातु ॥
ॐ शान्तिः । शान्तिः । शान्तिः ॥

Om! Bhadram karnebhih shrunuyaama devaah
bhadram pashyemaakshabhir yajatraah
sthirairangai stushtuvaagum sastanoobhih
vyashema devahitam yadaayuh
svasti na indro vriddhashravaah
svasti nah pooshaa vishva vedaah
svasti nastaarkshyo arishtanemih
svasti no brihaspatir dadhaatu.
Om Shaantih Shaantih Shaantih.

O Ye Gods! May we hear with our ears only what is auspicious. May we see with our eyes only what is auspicious. May we, who sing your praise, live our alloted span of life in perfect health and vigour. May Indra who is praised by the devotees, vouchsafe to us safety and well-being. May the all-knowing Pooshan grant us safety. May Garuda and Brihaspati grant us well-being. Om peace, peace, peace.

ॐ पूर्णमदः पूर्णमिदं पूर्णात् पूर्णमुदच्यते ।
पूर्णस्य पूर्णमादाय पूर्णमेवावशिष्यते ॥
ॐ शान्तिः शान्तिः शान्तिः ॥

Om Poornamadah poornamidam
poornaat poornamudachyate
poornasya poornamaadaaya
poornamevaavashishyate.
Om Shaantih Shaantih Shaantih.

The invisible is the Infinite, the visible too is the Infinite. From the Infinite, the visible universe of infinite extension has come out. The Infinite remains the same, even though the infinite universe has come out of it.
Om Peace Peace Peace.

2. Lord Vinaayaka
Om Ganeshaaya namah

Mahaaganapati has several names. The familiar ones are Ganapati, Ganesha, Vinaayaka, Gajaanana etc. He is the God of plenty, wisdom, good fortune, peace and spiritual success. Pleased by our prayers, He removes all obstacles in the path of any work we undertake. So He is called Vighneshvara. He stands for Om, for His figure with an elephant's trunk resembles the form of Om. Hence He is also called Pranava Svaruupa.

He represents perfect wisdom. He has an elephant head. We are all familiar with the story how He got the elephant head. But it has a great symbolic explanation. A common word for elephant in Sanskrit is 'gaja' Ga means the 'gati' or the final goal towards which the entire creation is moving. Ja stands for 'janma', birth or origin. Hence 'gaja' signifies God from whom the worlds have come out and towards whom they are progressing to merge in Him at the end. His large ears indicate continuous and intelligent listening to the teacher. We know how sage Vyaasa dictated the big book of Mahaabhaarata to Ganesha and Ganesha wrote down continuously without leaving a word and at the same time understanding the meaning fully. It shows how sharp His hearing was and how deep His concentration.

He has a long trunk. The trunk of an elephant can pick up a pin and at the same time, it can uproot a big tree. It means that He can handle any work big or small. If a poor and humble man prays, Ganesha fulfils his wants and if a demon challenges He destroys him. He is most compassionate but most powerful.

His vehicle is a small mouse. Mouse is small but not insignificant. If a lion is caught in a net it cannot escape, but if a mouse wants, it can cut asunder the net by its teeth and free the lion in no time. The mouse also represents desires. Desires are man's enemies. If man runs after desires he perishes. Ganesha sits on the mouse and controls it. It indicates that man should control desires fully.

Ganesha has four arms. He has a noose or rope in one hand. It signifies worldly attachments which make us suffer endlessly. Worldly attachments are a bondage like a rope.

The second hand holds Ankusha or goad. It represents anger. Just as the noose binds us, anger hurts us like a goad.

When our attachments and anger increase, life becomes miserable. The only way of escaping from the tyranny of these is to take refuge in God. It is better for us to surrender our attachment and anger to Him. When they are in His hands, we are safe. The third hand holds modaka — a sweet preparation. If we please Him by our good character and worship, He bestows happiness on us.

The fourth hand is in the blessing pose. He blesses the whole humanity. After all we are His children and He wants us all to be always happy and cheerful.

He has a large belly. It indicates that all created worlds are contained in Him. It also shows His ability to stomach and digest all types of experiences, good and bad.

गजवक्त्रं सुरश्रेष्ठं कर्ण-चामर-भूषितम् ।
पाशांकुशधरं देवं वन्देऽहं गणनायकम् ॥

Gajavaktram surashreshtham karna chaamara bhooshitam

*paashaankushadharam   devam   vandeham
                                 gananaayakam.*

I bow before, that God, who is the leader of Shiva's ghosts, whose face resembles that of an elephant, who is supreme among the deities, who sports ears that look like fans and who is armed with noose and goad.

एकदन्तं महाकायं तप्तकाञ्चनसन्निभम् ।
लंबोदरं विशालाक्षं वन्देहं गणनायकम् ॥

*Ekadantam   mahaakaayam   taptakaanchana
                                 sannibham
lambodaram   vishaalaaksham   vandeham
                                 gananaayakam.*

I bow down to the Lord of all, who is of one tusk, large body, whose complexion is like that of molten gold, who has a big belly and large eyes.

3. Lord Shiva
Om Shivaaya namah

Brahma, Vishnu and Maheshvara form the Trinity of gods. Each God has a particular responsibility. Brahma creates this universe, Vishnu maintains it and Shiva is responsible for the dissolution of the universe. The picture or image of Shiva shows him as a very handsome youth, white as camphor. His limbs besmeared with ashes are strong and smooth. He has three eyes — the third eye being on the forehead between the eye-brows. His third eye is the eye of knowledge. With His three eyes He sees the past, present and future. Once Paarvati, in a playful mood, closed His two eyes and lo, the entire world was plunged in darkness. To save the worlds from this predicament, Shiva willed a third eye in between His eye-brows, sending forth light, fire and heat. Later on He opened His third eye — normally kept closed out of infinite mercy for humanity — to burn up Kaamadeva, the god of Love. The three eyes of Shiva represent the sun, moon and fire. Shiva as the Lord of the universe rides on the bull of Dharma having the four feet of truth, purity, kindness and charity.

Shiva is snow-white in colour, which matches wonderfully with the background of the Himaalayas which is His abode.

A tiger skin forms His cloth. Tiger is symbol of desire. To show that He has complete mastery over desires He wears the tiger skin.

Shiva is the Lord of Yogis. He sits in deep meditation immersed in joy. He has Ganga on His head. It represents wisdom and purity.

There is a snake on His neck. It shows that He has no death. Even when He drank poison it didn't kill Him. It adorned His neck with a blue colour. And that is why He is called Neelakantha. He has a Trishula or trident in His hand. It is an important weapon of offence and defence, indicating that He is the Supreme ruler. Another hand holds Damaru. While doing Taandava dance, it produced the sound of Sanskrit syllables. So it represents alphabets, grammar and language itself.

वन्दे शंभुं उमापतिं सुरगुरुं
वन्दे जगत्कारणं

LORD SHIVA

वन्दे पन्नगभूषणं मृगधरं
　वन्दे पशूनां पतिं ।
वन्दे सूर्यशशांक वह्निनयनं
　वन्दे मुकुन्दप्रियं
वन्दे भक्तजनाश्रयं च वरदं
　वन्दे शिवं शंकरम् ॥

Vande shambhum umaapatim suragurum
　vande jagatkaaranam
vande pannagabhooshanam mrigadharam
　vande pashoonaam patim
vande soorya shashaanka vahninayanam
　vande mukundapriyam
vande bhaktajanaashrayam cha varadam
　vande shivam shankaram.

I bow down to the Lord Shiva, who is the consort of Uma, who is the Teacher of the celestials, who is the ultimate cause of the universe, who is adorned with snakes, who holds a deer, who is the Lord of beings, whose three eyes are the sun, the moon, and the fire, who is dear to Vishnu, who is the refuge of the devotees, who grants boons and who is all auspiciousness and who bestows peace.

अशनं गरलं, फणी कलापो
वसनं चर्म च वाहनं महोक्षः ।
मम दास्यासि किं किमस्ति शंभो
तव पादाम्बुज भक्तिमेव देहि ॥

Ashanam garalam phanee kalaapo
vasanam charma cha vaahanam mahokshah
mama daasyaasi kim kimasti shambho
tava paadaambuja bhaktimeva dehi.

O auspicious Lord, poison is your food, serpents your ornaments, animal hide your garment and an old bull your vehicle. What then can you give me? What indeed have you got to give! So grant me steadfast devotion to your lotus feet.

4. Lord Vishnu
Om Vishnave namah

Many temples are dedicated to Lord Vishnu. Srirangam and Trivandrum are very famous. Here the Deity is called Anantashayana — the Lord sleeping on a bed of serpent. After the dissolution of the universe and before the creation of the next universe the Lord sleeps on the bed of the great serpent called Ananta or Sesha floating on the ocean of milk. One of His legs is resting on the lap of His consort Lakshmi, who is gently pressing it. When He thinks of the next creation, a lotus springs forth from His navel along with God Brahma seated on it. After waking up, He instructs Brahma how to proceed with the work of creation.

The word Vishnu means 'one who pervades.' He pervades the whole universe. That is why we say, 'God is everywhere.' Another common name for Him is Naaraayana. Naaraayana means 'one who has made the hearts of human beings His abode.'

Lord Vishnu has four arms holding Shankha (conch), Chakra (discus), Gadaa (mace), and

Padma (lotus). The Shankha represents the five basic elements of the universe i e., Earth, Water, Fire, Air and Ether. Chakra stands for cosmic mind. Mind is swift and sharp like chakra. Gadaa indicates the Cosmic intellect and Padma indicates the evolving world. Just as the lotus is born out of water and unfolds gradually in all its glory, the world is also born of the causal waters and evolves gradually in all its splendour.

In the standing posture of Lord Vishnu, one of His hands is towards the feet and the other towards the devotee, as if the Lord is asking the devotee to surrender himself completely and take refuge at His feet so that He might give him the boon of freedom from fear.

नमोस्त्वनन्ताय सहस्रमूर्तये
सहस्रपादाक्षि शिरोरुबाहवे ।
सहस्रनाम्ने पुरुषाय शाश्वते
सहस्रकोटि युगधारिणे नमः ॥

Namostvanantaaya sahasra moortaye
sahasra paadaakshi shiroru baahave
sahasra naamne purushaaya shaashvate
sahasra koti yugadhaarine namah.

Salutation to that God with a thousand forms, having a thousand eyes, heads, feet and arms. Salutations to that Eternal Being called by a thousand names, and enduring through a thousand crore aeons.

शान्ताकारं भुजगशायनं पद्मनाभं सुरेशं
विश्वाधारं गगनसदृशं मेघवर्णं शुभाङ्गम् ।
लक्ष्मीकान्तं कमलनयनं योगिहृद्ध्यानगम्यं
वन्दे विष्णुं भवभयहरं सर्वलोकैकनाथम् ॥

*Shaantaakaaram bhujagashayanam padmanaabham suresham
vishvaadhaaram gaganasadrisham meghavarnam shubhaangam
lakshmeekaantam kamalanayanam yogihriddhyaanagamyam
vande vishnum bhavabhayaharam sarvalokaikanaatham.*

I bow down before Vishnu, the Lord of all worlds and the remover of all causes of fear. He is of blissful form. He lies on a serpent bed. He sports a lotus on His navel. The Lord of the celestials, He supports the whole cosmos.

His limbs are exquisite and His complexion is blue like that of the sky and the rain-cloud. The consort of Lakshmi, He has eyes rivalling the lotus. The yogis meditate on Him in their innermost heart.

5. Goddess Saraswati

Om Vaagdevyai namah

The Goddess of learning is called Saraswati because She gives (ti) the essence (saara) of our own Self (sva). She is the Shakti, the power and the consort, of Brahma the Creator. She is considered to be the personification of learning. She is the embodiment of Vidya (Education), Buddhi (Intellect), Smriti (Memory), Jnaana (Knowledge) and Prajna (Wisdom). She is also familiarly called Veenaapaani, Vaagdevi and Shaarada. Knowledge is opposite to ignorance. Ignorance is signified by dark colour and knowledge by white. That is why She is depicted as pure white in colour. She has four hands. She holds a rosary and a book in two of Her hands, and a veena with Her other two hands.

Being the Goddess of learning, it is but proper that Saraswati holds a book in her hand. The book represents all areas of secular sciences. The veena shows the need for the cultivation of fine arts. The rosary symbolises all spiritual sciences.

जय जय देवि चराचरसारे कुचयुगशोभित मुक्ताहारे ।
वीणापुस्तकरञ्जितहस्ते भगवति भारति देवि नमस्ते ॥

Jaya jaya devi charaachara saare
  kuchayuga shobhita muktaahaare
veenaapustaka ranjitahaste
  bhagavati bhaarati devi namaste.

Hail to Thee, Devi, who is the Essence of the universe, whose breasts are adorned with a garland of pearls, whose hands are fondling a veena and a book and who is Bhagavati and Bhaarati Devi.

या कुन्देन्दु तुषारहार धवला या शुभ्र वस्त्रावृता
या वीणावरदण्ड मण्डितकरा या श्वेत पद्मासना ।
या ब्रह्माच्युत शंकर प्रभृतिभिर्देवैः सदा वन्दिता
सा मां पातु सरस्वती भगवती निःशेष जाड्यापहा ॥

Yaa kundendu tushaarahaara dhavalaa
  yaa shubhra vastraavritaa
yaa veenaa varadanda manditakaraa
  yaa shveta padmaasanaa
yaa brahmaachyuta shankara prabhritibhir
  devaih sadaa vanditaa

saa maam paatu sarasvatee bhagavatee nihshesha jaadyaapahaa.

Goddess Saraswati is all white like the kunda blossom, the moon, snow, and pearl. She is dressed in pure white. While two of Her hands play the veena, the two other hands are poised to give boons, and award punishments as needed. She is seated on a white lotus. She is ever worshipped by all the celestials including Brahma, Vishnu and Maheshwara. May this Saraswati remove my obstacles and protect me.

6. Goddess Lakshmi

Om Lakshmyai namah

Lakshmi or Shri is the Goddess of wealth and fortune, power and beauty. According to the Bhaagavata puraana, during the churning of the milk ocean by the Devas and the Asuras for nectar, one of the auspicious gifts they got was Sri Lakshmi Devi.

Lakshmi is usually described as enchantingly beautiful and standing on a lotus and holding lotuses in each of Her two hands.

पद्मानने पद्मविपद्मपत्रे पद्मप्रिये पद्मदलायताक्षि ।
विश्वप्रिये विष्णुमनोऽनुकूले त्वत्पादपद्मं मयि सन्निधत्स्व ॥

Padmaanane padmavipadmapatre
   padmapriye padmadalaayataakshi
vishvapriye vishnumanonukuule
   tvatpaada padmam mayi sannidhatsva.

(O Lakshmi), lotus is your seat. Your limbs are delightful like the lotus creepers of earthly and heavenly regions. You love to abide in lotus, fond of the world you are and the world also is fond of you, you are always agreeable

to the wishes of Vishnu, (be pleased to) place your lotus foot in me; make my house your abode.

पद्मानने पद्मऊरु पद्माक्षि पद्मसंभवे ।
तन्मे. भजसि पद्माक्षि येन सौख्यं लभाम्यहम् ॥

Padmaanane padma-ooru
  padmaakshi padmasambhave
tanme bhajasi padmaakshi
  yena saukhyam labhaamyaham.

Oh lotus-eye Lakshmi! You are born of lotus. Your face is lovely like lotus. Your limbs are tender and smooth like lotus. (I entreat) you to bless me so that I will obtain happiness.

नमस्तेऽस्तु महामाये श्रीपीठे सुरपूजिते ।
शंखचक्र गदाहस्ते महालक्ष्मि नमोऽस्तु ते ॥
सर्वज्ञे सर्ववरदे सर्वदुष्ट भयंकरि ।
सर्वदुःख हरे देवि महालक्ष्मि नमोऽस्तु ते ॥

Namastestu mahaamaaye
  shree peethe surapoojite
shankha chakra gadaa haste
  mahaalakshmi namostu te.

Sarvajne sarvavarade
 sarva dushta bhayankari
sarva dukhahare devi
 mahaalakshmi namostu te.

Prostrations to you Goddess Mahaalakshmi, who is the great deluder, who is seated on the Shri Chakra, who is worshipped by the celestials and who sports in Her four hands the conch, the discus, the mace and the lotus.

Prostrations again to you, who are omniscient, who shower boons on the good and are a terror to all the wicked, and who remove all sorrows of devotees.

7. Guru.

Om Gurave namah

It is indeed a strange phenomenon that a human child has to depend on its elders for its survival, for a long period. No doubt all children are born with latent talents. But these talents have to be developed and guided in children by the teacher to achieve secular and spiritual perfection. So the teacher is the guide for every human being. The word 'Guru' consists of two letters gu and ru. Gu means ignorance and ru means one who removes it.

गुरुर्ब्रह्मा गुरुर्विष्णुः गुरुर्देवो महेश्वरः ।
गुरुस्साक्षात् परब्रह्म तस्मै श्री गुरवे नमः ॥

Gurur brahmaa gurur vishnuh
  gurur devo maheshvarah
gurussaakshaat parabrahma
  tasmai shree gurave namah.

Know the Guru to be verily Brahma himself. He is Vishnu, He is also Shiva. Know Him to be verily the Supreme Brahman, and offer thy adorations unto that peerless Guru.

ब्रह्मानन्दं परमसुखदं केवलं ज्ञानमूर्तिं
द्वन्द्वातीतं गगनसदृशं तत्त्वमस्यादि लक्ष्यम् ।
एकं नित्यं विमलं अचलं सर्वधीसाक्षि भूतं
भावातीतं त्रिगुणरहितं सद्गुरुं तं नमामि ॥

Brahmaanandam paramasukhadam
  kevalam jnaanamoortim
dvandvaateetam gaganasadrisham
  tattvamasyaadi lakshyam
ekam nityam vimalam achalam
  sarvadhee saakshibhootam
bhaavaateetam trigunarahitam
  sadgurum tam namaami.

Salutations to the true Guru who is the embodiment of the Bliss of Brahman and the bestower of supreme happiness, who is detached, knowledge personified and beyond duality, who is like the sky, and is indicated by such Vedic dicta as "Thou art That" and who is One, eternal pure, immovable, the witness of all the changes in the Buddhi (intellect), beyond all states and devoid of the three gunas.

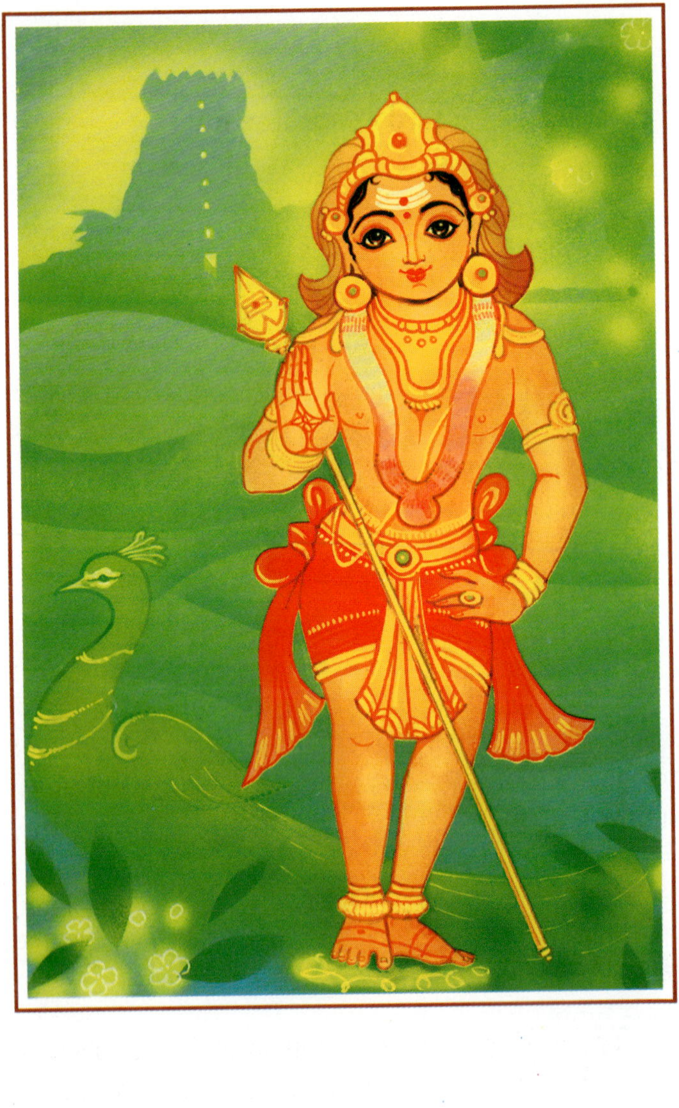

8. Lord Subrahmanya
Om Subrahmanyaaya namah

Lord Subrahmanya, familiarly called Muruga, is born of Shiva and Paarvati to destroy the demon Taarakaasura. He was appointed Commander-in-chief of the gods. With His matchless weapon, the shakti or lance, shining brilliantly like fire, He destroyed Taarakaasura. Being worshipped always as very young, He is also called Kumara. He is depicted as a boy either with one head and two arms or with six heads and twelve arms.

The word Subrahmanya means one who tends the spiritual growth of the aspirants. His six heads represent five sense organs and the mind. When these are controlled and sublimated, man becomes perfect.

The shakti or lance stands for knowledge and wisdom with which the demon of ignorance can be destroyed.

The peacock is His vaahana. It is shown as belabouring a snake with one of its legs.

The snake represents lust or lower desires. The peacock signifies the power of celibacy. By the power of celibacy man can put down lust or desires and become perfect.

पडाननं कुङ्कुमरक्तवर्णं महामतिं दिव्यमयूरवाहनम् ।
रुद्रस्य सूनुं सुरसैन्यनाथं गुहं सदा शरणमहं प्रपद्ये ॥

Shadaananam kumkuma raktavarnam
   mahaamatim divya mayoora vaahanam
rudrasya soonum sura sainya naatham
   guham sadaa sharanamaham prapadye.

I seek refuge for ever with the six-faced God of vermilion complexion, the son of Rudra, leader of the army of gods, who possessed of great intelligence, and mounted on a celestial peacock, ever resides in the cave of human hearts.

नमो नमस्ते गुह शक्तिधाम्ने
   नमो नमस्ते गुह शक्तिधर्त्रे ।
नमो नमस्ते गुह देवसेना
   भर्त्रे नमस्ते कुलभूषणाय ॥

Namo namaste guha shaktidhaamne
   namo namaste guha shaktidhartre

namo namaste guha devasenaa-
bhartre namaste kulabhooshanaaya.

Salutations to the Lord Subrahmanya, who is the abode of power, who holds the lance, who is the commander of the celestial hosts and who is the ornament of His divine family.

9. Sri Ramakrishna
Om Ramakrishnaaya namah

God takes birth from time to time in human form to teach mankind.

Sri Rama and Sri Krishna, are well-known examples of such a birth. In this age He was born as Sri Ramakrishna, in a village of Bengal. From childhood he had a great yearning for the vision of God. At the age of sixteen he became a priest in a Kali Temple at Calcutta. With single-minded devotion he prayed to the Divine Mother to reveal Herself. Pleased by his sincerity the Divine Mother appeared to him. After the vision of God, he was recognised as a great spiritual giant. Attracted by his spiritual power, people of all classees — men and women, young and old, educated and illiterate — all came to him for guidance. He specially trained a small band of young Sannyasins, who at his bidding took the vow that they would realise God by serving their fellow men. These disciples, guided by Swami Vivekananda, his chief disciple, started the Ramakrishna Math and Ramakrishna Mission

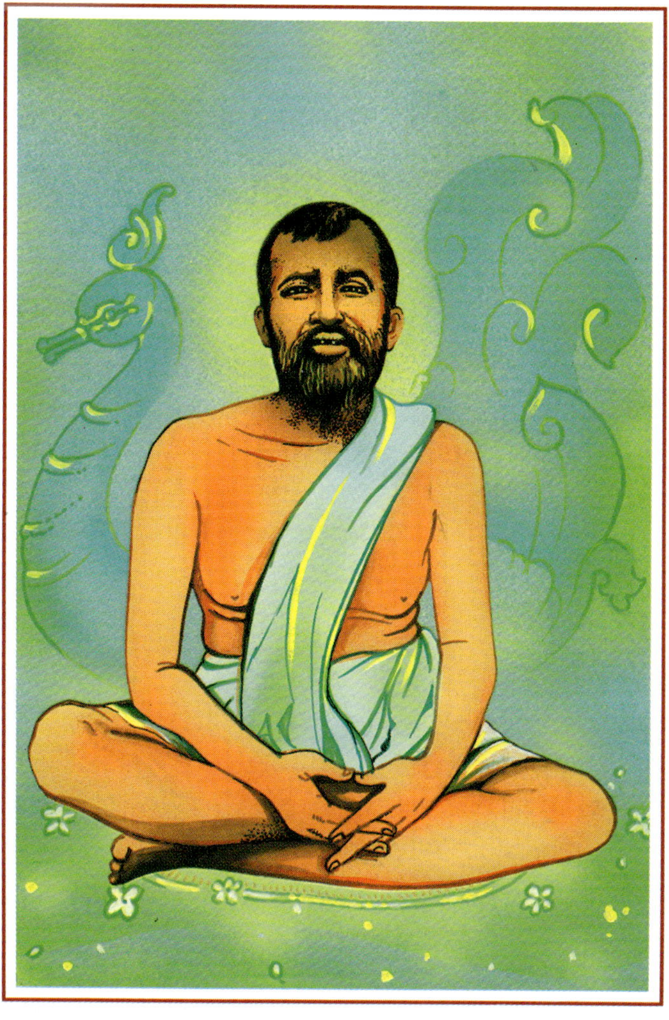

to spread the message of Ramakrishna. His teachings are very simple in language and encourage every one to seek God and lead a pure life. Praying to him brings us bliss and happiness.

ॐ ह्रीं ऋतं त्वमचलो गुणजित् गुणेड्यः
नक्तं दिवं सकरुणं तव पादपद्मं ।
मोहं कषं बहुकृतं न भजे यतोऽहं
तस्मात्त्वमेव शरणं मम दीनबन्धो ॥

Om hriim ritam tvamachalo gunajit
                                    gunedyah
naktam divam sakarunam tava
                              paadapadmam
moham kasham bahukritam na bhaje
                                    yatoham
tasmaat tvameva sharanam mama
                              deenabandho.

Om! Hreem! Thou art the True, the Imperturbable One, transcending the three gunas and yet adored for Thy virtues! Inasmuch as I do not worship day and night with yearning Thy compassionate lotus feet which destroy all ignorance, therefore, O Thou! friend of the lowly, Thou art my only refuge.

निरञ्जनं नित्यमनन्तरूपं भक्तानुकंपाद् धृतविग्रहं वै ।
ईशावतारं परमेशमीढ्यं तं रामकृष्णं शिरसा नमामि ॥

Niranjanam nityamananta roopam
bhaktaanukampaad dhrita vigraham vai
eeshaavataaram parameshameedhyam
tam raamakrishnam shirasaa namaami.

Thou art stainless, eternal and multiformed, but hast assumed a form out of Thy abounding grace to devotees. Thou the adored Lord of all, manifest as the Divine Incarnate, To Thee Ramakrishna, my obeisance with bowed head.

ॐ स्थापकाय च धर्मस्य सर्वधर्म स्वरूपिणे ।
अवतार वरिष्ठाय रामकृष्णाय ते नमः ॥

Om sthaapakaaya cha dharmasya sarva
                    dharma svaroopine
avataara varishthaaya ramakrishnaaya
                              te namah.

O Ramakrishna, founder of universal religion, and the embodiment of all world religions, to Thee the noblest of Divine Incarnations, I offer my Salutation